ACKNOWLEDGMENTS

To all friends, family and colleagues who support this effort in many special ways!

To Roy who fully supported all of my ideas with endless love.

Jastin is twelve years old and hears a lot of complaints from his friends about their grandmas and granddads - who don't know technology - always calling up to ask about how to find some button on the remote that came with their new television sets or how to work their new mobile smartphone or new tablet.

They laughed about how their grandparents would say things like - "Sonny – can you tell me how to program this "dagnabit" remote control so that I can tape my favorite show? I don't know why they make this stuff so confusing!" "What is this 'texting' thing? The screen is too small for me to type anything with just my thumbs." "What in the world is a website?"

Jastin's school friends also complain that now that they try to use the Internet and mobile smart phones too, the calls from Grannies do not stop coming, and as soon as they click on something that they shouldn't – bam - nothing else works!
"Sonny – HELP!!"

But Jastin is smart – his Nanna is Super Cybersecurity Grandma. That's the name he gave her because she knows all about how to work video recorders, smart phones, setting up networks, programming computers and working on the Internet. She can go to websites and stream videos from her cell phone straight to the television anytime. They don't have to wait until the shows come on TV, they can watch sports and a lot of other things – anytime, anywhere. Jastin's not sure what this "streaming" thing is, but it is different from watching the regular television that comes into the house over cable - and he thinks it is cool!
Jastin likes to call her **Super CeeGee** for short.

Super CeeGee teaches Jastin how to do all of these cool Internet things and sometimes now he can even show her "a thing or two" especially when she can't see the small smart phone screen! Sometimes her bi-focals don't work like they should - LOL!

Super CeeGee teaches all of these things because she wants Jastin and his friends to grow up to be special workers in the cybersecurity world.

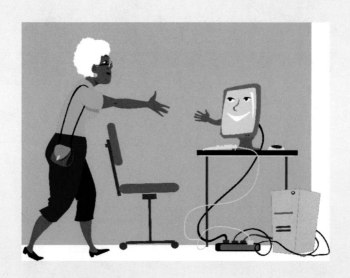

Jastin was so smart, that one day when Super CeeGee was traveling and not around, he decided to go to his computer and join a new club that he heard about from his school buddies. In school they were studying animals and he thought the club called *"Let's go hunting for Special Animals in Your Neighborhood"* – www.neighborhoodanimals.org would be fun. Joining the website would allow him to talk to his friends, meet new friends, post pictures of his special finds and where they were located, create avatars, and let everyone know about the special work that he was doing. This was going to be fun! He might even get extra credit from his teacher.

Jastin entered all of the information that the website asked for like his name and address, his age and date of birth, his parent's names and the name of the school he attends. Boy, was he having fun! He knew that his teacher would be proud of him. The website then gave Jastin instructions on how to roam his neighborhood and to take smart phone pictures of anything he saw that was interesting about animals and then to upload the pictures to the www.neighborhoodanimals.org website.

The next weekend Jastin did just that – he took pictures outside his home of squirrels, rabbits, and dogs with their owners. He took many pictures. He even took a picture of a snake crawling under his Dad's car. Everyone would really find that photo interesting. So back to the computer Jastin uploaded the pictures.

The other exciting thing about the website was that Jastin could talk to his friends from school. They would share things about their parents, sisters and brothers, and where and when they were going on vacation. They were having a blast sharing information and photos, never noticing that there were other people online who they didn't really know. Until one day when *strange things* started to happen.

Jastin received an email that said in the subject line *"Open This Email to Win the newest gaming Console - FREE"* -- of course he clicked on it because it sounded like a good offer. Jastin was sharing the gaming system at home with his brother and sister and really wanted one of his own. The email looked like it came from the familiar neighborhood animals' website.

All of a sudden Jastin's computer started to slow down and the mouse and keyboard did not work correctly. He could see the cursor moving on the screen without even touching the mouse. Someone had taken control of his computer. Then there was a big red flashing sign on the computer screen -

"YOU HAVE BEEN HACKED' @@##&&$%#@!

WE OWN YOU AND ALL OF THE FILES, PICTURES, PASSWORDS, FINANCIAL INFORMATION AND PROGRAMS ON YOUR COMPUTER –

YOU NEED TO PAY US **$2,000** TO GET ALL OF YOUR INFORMATION BACK"

Jastin was afraid to tell Super CeeGee because he knew that she told him over and over again to be "safe online" - - not to give out personal information, not to click on email links where he wasn't familiar with the sender and on and on and on. What would happen to his computer, smart phone and gaming privileges – it would be a long time before he would be online again. So he started with his parents, they may not be so hard on him.

Jastin's parents were **horrified**. All of the family photos from their vacations and ancestors were on the computer. There were years of information important to the family along with school work, banking, and financial data. It was all being held for ransom by someone in cyberspace who they couldn't even see. Jastin's parents called the police and the FBI to get help. Hearing this story all too many times before, law enforcement told them to "just go ahead and pay the ransom." It is too hard to find out, in the world of cyberspace, who was the cyber hacker. It would probably cost them more than $2,000 to track down the culprits. So that's what they did and the hackers released the computer access back to them all. Whew!!!

Super CeeGee came home to find out that all of this happened while she was away. Too bad the family didn't call her from the beginning because she could have warned Jastin about being the victim of what is called "phishing attacks." They are used in emails, and this all started with Jastin putting too much information on an Internet website that he wasn't familiar with.

Phishing attacks are named that because they are just like real fishing where someone throws out the bait on a fishing pole to catch a poor, unsuspecting fish and the fish bites the bait and gets reeled in.
Jastin fell for the bait!!!!!
So, with yet another family meeting, Super CeeGee went over some familiar cyber awareness topics.

Maybe you can help identify what Super CeeGee will cover - Do you know about the dangers of entering your personal information in a computer, clicking on emails that are not familiar, phishing, and not having a backup of your pictures and documents?

Jastin didn't listen to any of those lessons from Super CeeGee so now the family was out of **$2,000** and he was in **BIG** trouble.

Think of some other cybersecurity problems that Jastin might see in the future based on his actions online. They seemed like fun at the time, but will they cause more online problems?

Read the additional episodes about online predators, malware, cyberbullying, social networking, privacy, passwords, chat rooms, GPS and more... problems that may come his way!

Glossary

Cyberbully – A cyberbully tries to take advantage of, or hurt someone using online means, like, email, texting, chat rooms and social media.

GPS - A Global Positioning System is a tool that is built into many mobile phones, cars and computers that pinpoints where you are currently located. The tool is great for navigation but can also announce your whereabouts to unwanted people.

Malware – Apps and Software that run on your computer that are placed there by a hacker for malicious purposes.

Online predators – Bad people who show up online looking for children or other people to prey on for different reasons.

Passwords – Passwords are used to allow you to log on to a website or a system. You should never share your passwords with anyone and you should make sure that they are hard to guess.

Privacy – Privacy is something that online users think that they have. In reality, there is no privacy for online postings on social media sites, sending email, or chatting or sending messages. Everything in the digital world can be seen by anyone so it is important to never post personal information or photos that you would not want everyone (especially your Grannie) to see.

Ransomware – Bad software or (malware) that can stop people from accessing their pc, laptop, tablet or smart phone in essence putting a lock on files, pictures, data, contacts, and screens until a ransom is paid to the hacker.

Social Networking – Social Networking is the use of tools like Facebook, Twitter, Snapchat, Instant Messaging, and other programs online to communicate with friends, family and other people. It can be used for positive things, but can also be used inappropriately, e.g. for cyberbullying, posting comments online that are not true about someone, making racist remarks, or calling someone names.

Streaming – Streaming is a term used for delivering music or video to a television, radio, smart phone or computer. The video or music is being sent from a service provider to these devices. It is almost the same as watching a TV show but the video and music are coming to you over the Internet.

Made in the USA
Columbia, SC
25 July 2022

63957008R00018